WordPress For

Beginners:

A Visual Step-By-Step Guide to

Mastering WordPress

Table of Contents

Introduction

Congratulations on purchasing *WordPress For Beginners: A Visual Step-By-Step Guide to Mastering WordPress,* and thank you for doing so.

The following chapters will discuss how important it is to have your online presence and how you can do it in the right way. With its flexible and sophisticated nature, WordPress can be easy to learn if you have the right guide. With this book, you will have in-depth knowledge not only about the basics of WordPress but also about certain advanced technicalities that will help your website stand out from the others. Being the most popular CMS or Content Management System in today's world, WordPress has several benefits to offer, and you should not stay behind.

If you want to build your website and learn all the ways of customization, design, and play around with WordPress themes, then this book is just what you need. Even if you do not have any knowledge in programming or design, WordPress is such a platform that can take you a long way without any advanced knowledge. Another important thing that you are going to learn is how you can utilize the full benefits of SEO and how you can make your website rank higher. You will also learn how to manage your content and make it aesthetic.

Once you have gone through all the chapters, I am sure that you will be well-equipped to launch your website to beat the competition in your niche.

There are plenty of books on this subject on the market, thanks again for choosing this one! Every effort was made to ensure it is full of as much useful information as possible, and please enjoy it!

Chapter 1: What Is WordPress?

Whether you are developing a website for your big business or yourself as an individual, WordPress is the platform you should use. But if you want to know about WordPress on a more technical level, then it is a content management system or CMS, and it is also the most popular one in the market. A CMS is a tool that coordinates everything related to setting up and running a website, making it a breeze to maintain a website, especially for those who are not versed in the technicalities of programming.

The platform was founded back in 2003, and back then, it was nothing more than an offshoot of another project which went by the name of b2/cafelog. But today it has become an open-source software which has its own family of contributors spread across the world. The software originally started as a collaboration between Mike Little and Matt Mullenweg. After facing a lot of struggles and having its fair share of cold days, WordPress is now considered to be the best platform for anyone to create their website.

Why Should You Choose WordPress?

There is a myriad of benefits associated with opening your website with WordPress, and here we are going to discuss all of them so that you understand the platform's importance.

1. It has been in the market for quite a long time

I have already mentioned that WordPress is in the market for a long time now as it was established in the year 2003. In the initial days, the platform served as a tool for bloggers only, but now it has expanded its reach to several sectors. Today, it has become the go-to platform for all – programmers and businesses alike. If you think about the number of years this platform has been in the market, it is safe to say that it is not going anywhere in the coming years. Also, according to the stats, every day, almost 500 websites are created using WordPress.

Yes, of course, there are plenty of CMS like WordPress sprouting up daily. But are they reliable? No. It's because you never know if they will be up, in the long run. So, if you are using any of these newbie CMS, then you need to rethink your position because they can get shut down or acquired by some other competitor at any moment.

2. It is an open-source CMS

The meaning of being an open-source CMS is that the building code of the platform is free, and anyone can access it. But if you are thinking that it is going to make your domain vulnerable, then you are wrong; this is because relying on WordPress will only give your website an added layer of security. Also, you can edit the code of WordPress based on your requirements whenever you want. But in doing this, you also have to remember one thing, and that is not all of the changes that you make will be accepted by the team of WordPress. In case your changes are approved, you might even have to update it to the latest version.

3. The best SEO-friendly platform

Who doesn't want their website to be on top of the search engine results? But for that, your platform has to be SEO friendly. If domain optimization is something that you want, then WordPress will be your best friend. Your website will automatically become a favorite to all search engines the moment you set up your website on WordPress. But do you know the reason behind this? Well, the website has been made with clean codes of a high-standard, and it follows simple compliance. In short, WordPress generates semantic markups.

The highly logical design, coupled with the responsive nature of the website, makes it the best friend of all search engines. Also, you will get Meta tag keywords for each page on WordPress, and this paves the way for better search engine optimization.

4. You don't have to spend a dime on WordPress

You must be thinking that this is some kind of a joke but believe me, it's not! WordPress is totally free to its users, and the only investment that you will have to make is for web hosting and domain name. You will not have to pay a single penny for installing or downloading WordPress. You can even modify it as mentioned above, but that too won't require any additional costs. No matter what kind of website you have in mind, you can build it with the help of WordPress.

You will learn more about the domain and hosting later on in this book, but for now, you should know that the domain is basically an address with which people can reach your website just like they reach your house. On the other hand, just like you store all your things in your house, web hosting is something similar to that. It will house your website.

5. It provides easy customization

The main aim of WordPress is to help all those non-programmers and web designers to take matters into their own hands and develop their own websites. And that is why the platform has a very easy customization process as well. So, even if you do not have any prior knowledge on the subject of website creation, WordPress will be the best fit for you. There are plenty of themes or website templates to choose from, and all of these are free. Whether you are building your own online store or blog or any business portfolio, WordPress has just the right theme you need. The implementation of these themes is very swift, as well.

You can also get access to the premium themes for a small amount of money, and they come with pre-set layouts and detailed documentation, which can really kick-start your website in no time. Also, these themes have their own options through which you can customize the colors, change the background, upload your own logo, develop eye-catching sliders, and much more. And the best part is that you do not have to create any code for doing all of these things. You can also take the help of different plugins on WordPress to customize some of the functionalities. Plugins are something like apps, but they are specially meant for websites, and they can add different types of advanced features to your site like contact forms, analytics, social media buttons, and so on.

Also, you will get several premium plugins, just like in the case of themes that can take your site to the next level. If you want to know more about these advanced functions, keep reading, and I have kept an entire chapter reserved for it.

6. It is way easy to manage

There is an endless number of built-in updates in WordPress, and this entire system makes it easier for users to manage their content. So, whatever you want to do, you can do it from your admin dashboard itself, including updating your themes and plugins. Also, whenever there is a newer version of WordPress, you need not worry about anything as WordPress itself will send you notifications. So, updating your site can be done with the click of a button. You can also use separate plugins to keep a backup of your data so that it is not entirely lost under any circumstance whatsoever. You will also be able to manage your site on the go with the help of the mobile appl.

7. There are endless options to protect your site

Being the largest website-building and blogging platform in the entire world, WordPress often falls prey to spam attacks. Also, due to the availability of so many sites, WordPress is mostly targeted by these attacks. But on the bright side, the platform will also provide you with endless options to keep your content safe and secure. Firstly, you need to choose a secure theme and also get a security back-up plugin. You will get both free and paid options for these services, but before you choose to install any of it, you need to read all the reviews of the plugin. You should also keep backups of your website to your local computer or your hard drive so that you can have something to fall back on.

8. It can handle different types of media

If you thought that you are getting all of these features simply for writing text, then you need to know that WordPress comes with a built-in media uploader. So, you can also insert images, videos, and audio files. Thus, it is an all-in-one package. Moreover, you can embed Instagram photos, YouTube videos, Soundcloud audio, and Tweets as well. And all of this can be done by simply pasting the link in the post editor.

What Can You Do With WordPress?

If you are wondering as to what are the websites that you can build with WordPress, then let me give you a walkthrough on this topic. You can build everything starting from the simplest of websites to complex eCommerce marketplaces, but here are some of the major categories of websites that are usually made with WordPress.

Blogs

If you ask around, you will find that most bloggers started their journey with WordPress. The most common reason for this is that when you are just starting out, you are a newbie with zero knowledge, and the WordPress community will give you all the support you need in this matter. The forum of WordPress is where you can get all the answers to your questions and that too in a very less amount of time. Also, when someone starts a blog, one of their major concerns is regarding the design and how to make it catchy. That is something you can do with WordPress in the blink of an eye. Also, later on, when your blog starts performing well, monetizing your website will not be a problem with WordPress.

A Business Website

Yes, you have heard it right! WordPress is not only suitable for blogs but also for business websites. The primary reason is obviously its manageable nature, even for a layman. Along with that, the content management system of WordPress will make it possible for you to manage both your website and your blogs. You can cut off the costs of hiring a separate website designer if you simply make use of the professional themes of WordPress. The plugins of the platform can be used to include several complex business functionalities to make everything more efficient. Also, one of the most important prerequisites of building the best business website is to ensure that it is mobile-friendly; otherwise, it will drive away half of your customers. With WordPress, you can stay assured about that too.

An Online Store

According to the stats, 45.4% of the total number of websites in today's world is eCommerce platforms, and with WordPress, you can get full control over your website. Also, you can combine your store with a variety of other pages like portfolios, blogs, and so on. It is possible to integrate several modern services with the help of WordPress alone, and all of this has made it the number one choice for most people.

Sell Online Courses

With the freelance market booming and people becoming more and more inclined towards remote working opportunities, selling online courses have also gained a lot of momentum. If you are not in for hiring a website developer for a full-time position, then WordPress will no doubt be your best friend in terms of endless customization and scalability. The plugins will basically do everything for you. If you are concerned about SEO, simply get Yoast SEO. If you want to capture leads, then leave it all to Salesmate. MailChimp is there to look into the various aspects of email marketing, and the list is endless. If you get a hold on the immensely large database of plugins, selling your courses through a WordPress site will be your best option.

Now that you have a basic idea about WordPress, the upcoming chapters will teach you how you can set up your own website.

Chapter 2: Installing and Upgrading WordPress

Before you dive deeper into the world of making your own website, you first need to learn how to install WordPress and also ensure that you have the latest version of it. Also, as already mentioned in the previous chapter, WordPress keeps upgrading its software from time to time. So, you need to be able to upgrade it as well when the time comes. This usually happens after every 120 days, but this is only an approximate count. Once you have figured out all of this stuff, you will have a strong foundation.

In this chapter, you will learn how you can install WordPress in a step by step manner. These installation steps are of utmost importance, and those who do not understand this are the ones who later on face server-related issues and other problems on the back-end. So, on completing this chapter, you will have a basic overview of all the processes involved in WordPress installation and upgrade.

Things You Need Before Installing WordPress

Before we move on to the topic of the actual installation, you need to have certain things which are; you can say, the prerequisites. You will need –

- A domain name
- A WordPress-friendly web hosting company

First, you need to understand what a domain name is. Just like your house has an address, your website needs one too, and your domain name serves a similar function. There is also a term known as IP address, but they are all numbers. For example, you might be having an IP address like this – 65.145.32.2 But remembering this number combination for every website you visit is quite a task and is difficult too. So, this problem can be solved with the help of domain names, for example, Netflix.com. This is way easier to remember than an assortment of numbers.

There are several registrars from where you can get your domain name. Also, you need to keep in mind that you need both domain names and web hosting to start your website. You can get both of them either from the same company or from different companies. Getting both from the same company will save you a lot of hassle as you can manage them both in the same place.

Bluehost is mainly used by people when it comes to setting up a WordPress site because they are not only a recommended provider for WordPress websites, but they are also one of the biggest hosting companies across the globe. Also, with Bluehost, your domain will be free, and you do not have to pay anything extra for it. Their hosting plans are affordable too. But apart from Bluehost, you will also get other options like HostGator, SiteGround, QuickInstall, and so on.

Step-By-Step Guide to Installing WordPress

Here, I have mentioned steps to install WordPress on different hosting platforms so that you get a basic idea of how it is done.

Steps to install WordPress on Bluehost

The first name that anyone will give you regarding WordPress hosting is Bluehost, and this is because the company literally knows WordPress to its core. Their installation process is also very friendly and suitable even for a layman to perform it on your own.

- The moment you sign up with Bluehost, your WordPress account will be installed on your domain name. This is done through an automatic process.
- The next time you log in to your account on Bluehost, click on the 'My Sites' tab and there you will be able to see your WordPress site listed.
- If you want to access the admin area of your WordPress site, all you have to do is click on the button named 'Log in to WordPress.' If you want to install WordPress on multiple sites, you can do it with Bluehost but not with the Basic Plan. Apart from that, every other plan will allow you to do so. You can then use their hosting plans on an unlimited number of sites.
- Now, once you reach the tab of 'My Sites,' you will see that there is a separate option called 'Create Site.' Click on that option. Once you do that, the installation wizard for WordPress will

be launched, and it is guided by Bluehost itself. Your site title is mandatory to proceed, and you will also have the option to add a tagline, but it is not compulsory for you to do so.

- After that, click on the Next button.
- Then you will have to choose the domain name for your website. But in case you have already purchased it, there will be a dropdown menu from where you can choose the name. Later on, you can add more domain names if you want, and all you have to do is visit the Domains tab, and it will be present on your dashboard.
- There is a place for your directory path. When you have selected your Domain name, you do not have to fill this option of Directory Path as Bluehost will do it for you. At the time of installation, a few options of important plugins will be shown to you in case you want to install them.
- Click on the Next button when you are done with all of the stuff.
- In a few moments, your WordPress site will be installed, and you can see all the details on your screen.

- Also, emails will be sent to your registered email id regarding this installation.
- The next time you click on the login button, you will be taken to the admin area of your site.

Steps to install WordPress on HostGator

HostGator is another of the shared hosting companies that beginners approach. You will be able to get your site up and running in just a few minutes with them.

- The first step is obviously to make an account with HostGator and then log in to your account. Go to your dashboard, and from there, you will get a separate section by the name of 'Software.' Under this section, click on the option named 'QuickInstall.'
- The moment you click on it, you will be directed to the next screen where you have to select WordPress. The installation wizard will launch upon clicking.

- Similar to the process of Bluehost, here too, you will have to enter your domain name and along with that a directory path.
- You can leave the directory path blank and click on the Next button.
- Then, in the next window, you will have to enter some details about your WordPress site. Some of these details are your admin username, your site's title, and email address for the admin, and also your first and last name.
- When you enter the email, you need to be careful about the fact that this email is the one where you will be getting your password reset email. So, make sure you enter an email that is secure and fully accessible to you.
- Once you have entered all the details asked, there is an Install button on which you have to click to complete the process.
- Then the installer will install WordPress as a background application, and when the process is done, you will get a message saying that the process was successful, and your user name and password will also be mentioned.

- The next step is for you to access the admin area by clicking on the Login button that appears on the window.

Steps to install WordPress on SiteGround

The highly optimized plans for hosting, along with the super-responsive support, make SiteGround popular among beginners. If you are in search of a pain-free installation procedure, then SiteGround will be your best friend. In fact, your hosting dashboard is from where you can directly install WordPress. There are two different methods which you can use, and I have explained both so that you can make your choice accordingly.

Method 1 – As a New User

A welcome popup box will appear on your screen if you have signed up on the website as a new user. This will appear the moment you login for the first time. On the window, it will be asked whether or not you want to set up your website now.

- In that option, you have to select the option which states start a new website and then proceed with the rest of the steps.
- The installation wizard will then be launched.
- There, all the installation details will be asked of you.
- A username for the admin, your email address where you want to receive all the important stuff, and a password will have to be inserted in this window.
- Once you have entered all these details, click on the Confirm option.
- After that, several other options to enhance your website will be shown to you, but I advise you to do all of that later on when you have a better grip on all enhancements of WordPress.
- There will be a Complete Setup button, and you have to click on it. WordPress will be installed in the background while you can do other work, although it takes only a while. Once the installation is done, a successful message will be displayed on the screen.
- A green button with the text 'Proceed to the Customer Area' will come on the screen, and

you have to click on it. There you will find a 'My Accounts' tab, and you will find your site there.

- If you want to enter your admin area, then all you have to do is click on the option – 'visit admin panel.'

Method 2 – As an Existing Customer

When you have your hosting account on SiteGround, installing WordPress is like a cakewalk. You can do it anytime and anywhere. Go to your cPanel dashboard, which is an interface that manages your entire account, and proceed with the following steps.

- There is a separate section named 'Auto Installers', and this is located quite towards the bottom of the page. So, you have to scroll down in order to find the section. Then, once you reach that part, click on WordPress.
- There is a preprogrammed auto-installer script that will be launched the moment you click on this option. From there, you will find the Install button, and you have to click on it.

- After that, you need to select your domain name and also your website protocol.
- Have you already enabled your SSL certificate? If yes, then you will have to set your protocol as https, but if you haven't, then HTTP will do just fine. Later one when you enable the certificate, you can convert it to https.
- After that, you will get more options where you have to enter details like your username, email address, site title, and password. There will also be some more additional options from where you can select the plugins, language, and so on. You can either keep them unchecked, or you can also choose options based on your preference.
- Then, lower down, you will find an option named WordPress starter. Make sure that you have checked it because it is a huge savior for beginners. You will be introduced to all the post-installation steps that are required to set up your site.
- Finally, you will find the Install button, and you need to click on it after completing the above-mentioned steps. A success message will be

displayed on your screen when the installation process is completed.

- You will also find a link on your screen that will directly forward you to the admin area.
- The moment you click on the link, you will not only be forwarded to your dashboard, but the Setup wizard will also be launched. If you want to proceed, then click on Start Now.

These were three of the main hosting providers and their procedures. The rest of them also follow a similar procedure, but it is recommended that you stick to these.

A Guide to Safely Upgrade WordPress

Are you feeling confused as to where to start or which option to select if you want to upgrade WordPress? Then you have come to the right place as I have spoken all about WordPress here in this section.

For starters, you need to understand why is it so essential to upgrade WordPress whenever a new version is launched. This is mainly because of security reasons. If you are running your website on an outdated version of WordPress, you are automatically making it more prone to hackers. Developers from all over the glove maintain WordPress programming. They include new features, fix bugs, and also remove any type of security vulnerability every once in a while. If the newer version is not that much of a big release, then this upgrade often happens automatically. Unless and until you are using a managed hosting for WordPress, you will have to learn how to do this upgrade manually if you want your WordPress to stay up to date.

The first step to upgrading your WordPress is to create a complete backup of your website. Even if you are using a separate plugin for it, you need to have the backup stored somewhere else just to be safe. This means everything is starting from your database to core WordPress files, and even your media should be saved.

Once you have created the backup, there are two methods that you can follow to upgrade WordPress. The first method is to do it with the built-in system.

All you have to do is visit the Updates page from your admin dashboard, and you will have the options there.

The second method is to do it manually. For this, you will have to take the help of FTP.

- Start off by downloading the newer version.
- The application will be downloaded in a zip format from which you have to extract the actual file.
- Then you have to open your FTP client to perform the following steps.
- Connect to your website. Then, you have to go to the files that you have just extracted.
- Your website's root folder will be present in the column of remote files. All the folders and files of your WordPress are present in this file, and this is usually named after your domain name or public_html.
- Open the folder and select all the files: Right-Click and select Upload.
- Since the older version of some of the files is present on your device, a dialog box may pop up asking what to do with them. There, you have to select Overwrite. Thus, you can stay

assured that all the older versions have been removed with these newer files.

- Once the process of upload is done, go to your admin area again.
- Sometimes, WordPress requires a separate database upgrade, and if the case is so with you, then you will see a notice on your dashboard. Click on the 'Upgrade WordPress Database' option.

Once you have followed all these steps, your WordPress upgrade will be completed successfully. But make sure every functioning is normally happening without any glitch. Also, review the Settings option from your admin area and check for any abnormality.

Chapter 3: Understanding Your Dashboard and Settings

Once you have installed WordPress, it is time for you to go out and explore other things starting with the Dashboard and Settings. If you look at the left-hand side of your screen, you will notice that there is a Navigation menu.

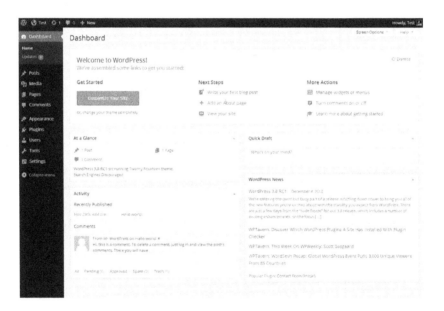

In that Navigation menu, there are separate options of Dashboard and Settings, and that is how you reach them.

All about the Dashboard

But in usual cases, the moment you log in, the first thing that you see on your screen will be your Dashboard as in the screenshot here. All the statistical information about your site is amalgamated in a gist format and displayed on your Dashboard. It is basically a snapshot of all the important information about your site. You can also find the updates for your plugins or WordPress development on your dashboard.

All the different sections that you see on this Dashboard, for example, the Right Now, Incoming Links, Recent Drafts, Recent Comments, and so on, all of these are known as widgets. If your WordPress is a newly installed one, then the sections will appear in two columns on your screen. But on the top right corner of your Dashboard screen, you will find a tab named Screen Options. Click on it. It is from here that you can adjust the number of columns, and you can keep it anywhere from one to four. In this tab, you will also get an option with which you can completely turn off the Widgets if you want by unchecking the box.

You can also rearrange the Widgets according to your wish by dragging them with the cursor. If you don't want the entire Widget to be visible, you can choose to collapse them as well, and in that case, only the title of the Widgets will be visible to you. On the right-hand corner of the title will be the down arrow, which you can use later on to see the contents of the Widget. In some cases, you can get configurable options for the Widgets, but this is only valid for a few of them like Incoming Links. If you are thinking as to how to access this option, then all you have to do is hover your cursor over the right-hand arrow, and the Configure link will show itself.

Now that you have an overall idea of your Dashboard, let us move on to the Settings. You will be able to control almost every aspect of your website from here. Apart from the general options, your number of options in settings might increase with the addition of plugins. There are a lot of things to discuss in this part, and so, we have divided it into several parts.

General Settings

First, let us start with General Settings.

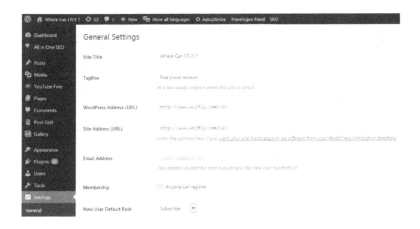

The first few options of this General Settings are pretty clear and basic. The first thing that you will see is the title of your site, and then there is the Tagline. After that comes the URLs, all of which were selected at the time of installation. The Tagline is nothing but a brief description of what your site is about, and so if you hadn't entered it at the time of installation, you could do so now. But remember that this tagline will be displayed to your audience somewhere close to your title. So, you need to keep it short and catchy and yet quite conclusive. At the end of the day, the position where your tagline will be displayed depends entirely on the Theme that you choose.

There are two other options in the basic General Settings, and these are New User Default Role and Membership. These options become crucial for anyone who has started a group blog or a blog that is managed by multiple people. Some of the basics about user roles are as follows –

- Subscribers do not have much freedom, and they can basically only edit their own profiles.
- The ones who can write posts and publish them are the authors.

- The contributors are those who can write posts, but they cannot publish them. They can simply give their posts to the Editor and then wait for the approval.
- Editors like authors can write posts and pages and also publish them. They have an extra role too. They can edit posts by other authors too.
- But there is only one role which can do it all, and it is that of the administrator.

But you also have to keep in mind that all of these roles are only meant for registered users. Any unregistered user on your website will be considered as a visitor only, and they cannot play any role on your website.

The remaining options in the panel of General settings are those of date and time. You can select the format of your date that you prefer and also set your local time zone in order to display the correct time. If you are using a calendar archive widget, then you will have additional settings, and that is the Week Starts On option. This, as the name says, decides on which day the week starts for you, and you can set it based on your preference.

Writing Settings

As you may have guessed already, this Settings option handles everything related to the WordPress editor. The first three options specifically deal with the Page Edit and Post screens. The TinyMCE editor is the one that is used by WordPress. Normal markup is present in the HTML view of the editor although, there is an automatic conversion of the line breaks. No matter which view you are using, the number of lines on the screen is what determines the post box size. The WordPress editor can handle emoticons, too, and this is determined by the next two options in the Settings panel.

When you have just installed your WordPress, you probably don't have any Default Category. Your links and posts and WordPress require you to assign them to at least one particular category. And in this Settings option, you can select the Default Category to which your posts will get assigned the moment you publish them.

If you are into remote publishing, then the next options are for you. In case you love blogging on the go, you will have to enable one of the protocols in this Settings panel, either the XML-RPC one or the Atom. But in case you are not going to do anything remotely, then you should keep these options unchecked; otherwise, you might end up inviting the hackers.

Reading Settings

Once you are done with the Writing Settings, now it is time for you to have a look at the Reading Settings. The main aim of these settings is to regulate the appearance of your posts to your visitors. Here, you can select the overall appearance of your website. If you want your recently published posts to appear on your Home Page, then this is where you can do it all.

Then comes the option of Blog Pages. With this option, you can decide the number of posts that you want to display on each page. This includes the search results, archive pages, and of course, the home page. If your aim is to make your subscribers click on your posts to read it all, then you can minimize the posts to only a small summary. But when you choose to display the summary to your visitors, you have to let go of the HTML formatting. This means all your images and lists will disappear, and if your content still makes sense after that, then you can choose this feature; otherwise, it is better to avoid it.

Discussion Settings

All handling of trackback and comments is done through the Discussion Settings.

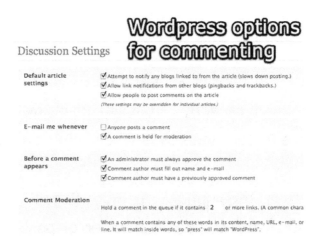

Whether you want to allow the trackbacks and comments or not is decided through this Settings panel. You can also choose how they are moderated. You can also fix things like how you prefer to get the notifications when someone comments on your post. You can also decide whether you want to display the avatars of the commenters. This is basically a screen containing a lot of options.

- **Default article settings –** This is the first section of the Discussion Settings. This setting actually refers to both pages and posts. The default options for any new pages or posts you publish are as follows, but you can change them at your own will –
  - If your blog has the mention or link to any other blog, then WordPress will notify those blogs before posting your content.
  - The next option allows you to decide whether or not you want others to pingback to your content.
  - The next option is regarding commenting, and it decides whether people can openly comment on your pages and posts. But you

have to remember that this applies to new posts only and not the old ones.

- **Comment email notifications** – This section consists of two options, and both of them are actually checked by default. For every comment that is posted, the author of the post will receive a notification, and if you want to stop this, then you have to uncheck the box. Also, if a comment is held for moderation, you will receive an email for that, too, and this email will be sent to the email id that is mentioned in the General Settings.

- **Comment moderation** – This section is all about determining which comments should be stopped for the purpose of moderation. This means that the moment someone posts on a comment on your website, it will not go up immediately. Instead, it will be added to a queue of comments in your admin area where you will have the power to approve or disapprove them. So, you can either choose that every comment should be sent to the admin for moderation. But this is not the default option as it often slows down the process of discussion. But what you can do is that you can choose to allow a comment only if the author has a comment that has been previously approved. Spam comments are usually those which contain a lot of links and so if someone makes a comment containing more than two links, then it will be automatically held for moderation by WordPress. But apart from the links, you can also specify other things like IP addresses or even words, the presence of which will send the comments directly to moderation. If you already know about keywords that tend to start debatable discussions or controversies, then you can include them in the list, and the comments will not be directly posted.

Media Settings

Then comes the Media settings through which you can select the dimension of your uploaded videos and images. You should always choose the default size of your images keeping in mind the layout of your website. For example, if your layout is of fixed-width type and supposes, your post area has a width of 600 pixels, then your picture size should have a maximum width of 600 pixels as well. You can also choose to turn off the auto-discovery option from here, as this usually tries to embed the videos whenever some link is posted in your content. At the bottom of this Settings screen, you can change the directory of your uploaded content.

Privacy Settings

There are only two options in this Settings panel. Here you have to choose whether you want to allow your website to be visible to search engines or only to visitors. If you choose to block the search engines, then you will also not be able to ping linked blogs.

Permalinks

If you want a custom URL, then you can do so on the Permalinks page. This comes of great help, especially if you want to improve the SEO performance of your site. You can change the structure of your permalinks at any time, and there is no limitation to that. But if your permalinks start with category names or post names, you can face certain problems in performance.

Chapter 4: How to Manage Your Content With WordPress?

There are several ways in which you can categorize, organize, and archive your content with WordPress. Within the software, you will get an option with the help of which you can keep your archived content categorized in a chronological manner. This entire process will also benefit your audience because now, they can access any content they want in the blink of an eye. Whatever you publish on your website can be accessed by your readers based on date and category, and this is enabled by the MySQL and PHP technology used by WordPress. With every post or page you publish, this process of categorization does not have to be done separately. WordPress will do it automatically for you.

In this chapter, you will learn everything about content management and how WordPress can help you with it. You will learn how to make tags and categories and also how you can make the best out of the Permalink system that is already present in

WordPress. Thus, after completing this chapter, you will now be able to make your site SEO-friendly. So, if you want to build an informative and dynamic website, this chapter will teach you how to do it, so sit tight and read on.

How to Archive Your Content With WordPress?

Whenever you are about to publish a new post on your website, you will have to assign a category to that particular post. When you do this, you are paving the way for an effective archiving system that your audience can use to find the posts of their choice. As already mentioned earlier, the published articles are also categorized on the basis of date so that you can access something easily that was published at a certain point in time. When you visit such an Archive page, you will notice that the months of various years are listed, and when you click on one of those months, all the posts published in that month will be revealed. Those articles are all in the form of clickable links, so if you want to read that article, all you have to do is click on the title.

But the date is not the only option in front of you when it comes to categorizing your content. So, the different types of archival categorization of content are explained below –

- **Categories** – To keep all the relevant topics together, you can create categories accordingly and based on a theme. You do not necessarily have to do it based on time. It can be something like Hotel Reviews, Destination Guides, and so one depending on your niche. This is a very popular way of categorization and very effective too.

- **Tags** – Tags are basically micro-keywords. Tagging your posts is also quite a nifty method of categorization. All the related content can be drilled down in no time, and this is also a plus point for SEO.

- **Date** – Whenever you are publishing some new content, it is auto-categorized based on its date.

- **Author** – If your website has multiple authors contributing to the posts, creating an author based archive is also essential.

- **Keyword** – There is a built-in keyword functionality in WordPress that will allow you to search relevant content just with the help of the keyword of your choice.

- **Attachments** – All the videos, photos, and documents are uploaded to the built-in media library of WordPress, and you can build an archive here as well.

How to Build Categories?

The main aim or topic of a post you make on your website is what makes the category too. Thus, if you want to file your posts into various subjects, the categories come of great help. This also enhances user experience as your audience can now navigate through your blog without any hassle. So, when you assign the categories, your visitors can simply click on one of those categories and reach the posts they were looking for. But these categories that you plan to create can be shown in two locations, and they are as follows –

- The first one is the body of your post itself. In most of the themes that WordPress has, the category is present just below the title of the post. One post can be filed in multiple categories, as well.

- The second place is the sidebar. If you have the Categories widget installed, then your sidebar will be showing all the categories that you have on your website. Your audience will then be able to click on any of those categories and visit the posts listed under them.

Apart from the categories, there are subcategories, as well. This makes the process even more refined. There will be a parent category within which the rest of the related subcategories will be listed. There will be a separate Manage Categories option on your Dashboard, and there you can see all your categories and subcategories clearly mentioned.

So, to start the discussion of categories, here are certain things that you need to learn.

Steps to Change the Name of a Category

When you have just installed WordPress, the default category option selected by WordPress is uncategorized. This means there will be a generic classification of your posts until and unless you make it specific by changing the name of the category.

But when you are choosing the name of your Default Category, you have to make sure that it completely aligns with the idea of your blog. This is because of it will kind of act like a failsafe. For example, if you forgot to assign any Category to a post that you have just published, it will be put under the Default Category no matter what its name is. So, the name must be selected in such a way that no matter what you put in it, the name correlates to the post.

So, if you want to change the name of a category, these are the steps that you have to follow –

Step 1 – Go to your Dashboard because that is where you will get all the options. From there, Select Posts and then click on Categories. The page will open, and here you will find all the options and tools that are essential to set up a new category or edit the name of an existing one.

Step 2 – Now, you need to click on that category, which you want to edit. If it is the Uncategorized one, then simply click on the title, and the page of Edit Category will open.

Step 3 – In the Name Text box, you will have to type in the name of the new Category. Then you will also have to edit the Slug, that is, the word that will be displayed on the web address of that page.

Step 4 – Then, there is an option to select the Parent Category. This will be applicable to you only if you are changing the name of a Subcategory and not a Category. If it is a Category, then you have to select None in the Parent Category box.

Step 5 – The next step is optional. Here, you can type a small description of your Category. This description can be used to remind you of the idea behind this Category. In some of the themes, there is an option to show the description of your Category to the audience, and this usually is helpful to the audience.

Step 6 – Once you have made all the changes, now it is time for you to click on the Update button. Everything that you have edited will be saved.

Steps to Create New Categories

As you continue to expand your blog, you will eventually require more than one Category, and so, you need to learn how to create them. There is no limitation to the number of Subcategories and Categories you can have on your blog, and so you can keep expanding.

Follow these steps and create a new Category in just a few minutes.

Step 1 – Firstly, go to your Dashboard. From there, you again have to click on the Posts option from where you will get Categories. Click on it. This step is similar to changing the name of an existing Category.

Step 2 – Once the Category page opens, on the left-hand side, you will see an option Add New Category. You have to click on this option.

Step 3 – In the Name Text Box that pops up, you need to enter the name of the New Category that you want to form. For example, you want to create a Category in which you will post all Itineraries; then, you can name the Category as Destination Itineraries.

Step 4 – Then, you have to go to the Slug text box and enter the name that you want in the web address. You can manually enter something here, but in case you leave it blank, the name will be based on your Category name.

Step 5 – If you are creating a sub-category, then you have to select the Parent Category from the drop-down menu. But in case this is a Category, then select None.

Step 6 – Here, too, you can type a description for the category you are creating.

Step 7 – At last, you can click on the Add New Category button, and that's it! You have your new Category created, and now you can assign your posts to it.

In case you want to delete any of your Categories, that is easy too. All you have to do is simply hover the pointer of your mouse over the title of the Category. In a while, you will see that a Delete Link has appeared. But you need to remember that if you delete a category, it doesn't mean that you are deleting the posts in it. When the Category is deleted, all the posts that were present in it will now be assigned to the Uncategorized one or whatever Category you have set as your Default one.

All About Customizing Permalinks

Whenever you make a new post on WordPress, it will be assigned a Permalink or web address. This

Permalink is usually present in four places in a typical WordPress post, and these are as follows –

- Your blog post's title
- At the bottom of the post with the Comments link
- In most themes, the Permalink is also present below the post
- In the sidebar for Recent Posts with the title of the post

A Permalink, when given to someone else, will direct that person to your post. So, no matter how many edits you make to your post, your Permalink will remain the same until and unless you willingly change it. In default cases, the posts are given Permalinks based on their ID number, but this is not advisable. You should give a makeover to your Permalinks if you want your website to perform well.

When you convert the Permalinks to the name of your post, they not only look better but are also preferred by the Search Engines. If you want to choose the format of your Permalinks, it is quite an easy procedure. You have first to select Settings and from their click on the Permalinks option. The page of Permalinks Settings will open.

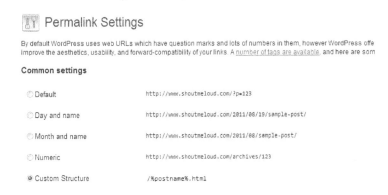

The different options of Permalinks and their meanings are explained below –

- **Default** – These are the Permalinks that Wordpress creates automatically for you. The URL is composed of an ID number that is assigned to each post.

- **Day and Name** – These are the ones that look better than the default ones because they have a post name along with the day, month, and year on which the post was published.

- **Month and Name** – This is similar to the previous one. The only difference is that the day is not mentioned in the Permalink, and only the month, year, and title of the post are present.

- **Numeric** – There is a numeric value or ID which is assigned to every post on WordPress, and this numeric Permalink is the one where that number of ID is present.
- **Post Name** – There is also an option called Post Name, and in this, only the title of the post will be mentioned in the Permalink.
- **Custom Structure** – If none of the above-mentioned types appeal to you, then you can always customize your Permalinks on WordPress. You can use variables or tags of your choice to create a customized Permalink.

Things to Do Before You Launch Your Website

Now, before you launch your website on WordPress, you also need to make sure of certain things for better performance, and they are mentioned below –

- **Always have a backup solution** – Just like you get car insurance before you drive your car, a backup solution for your WordPress has a similar function. Even if something goes wrong with your site, you will always have your backup. There are so many backup plugins that you will get on WordPress, both free and paid. But one thing that you should ensure is that the backup must be stored in some cloud, and it should also be done automatically to save you the hassle. Also, you should keep the backup in multiple locations, and apart from the cloud storage, keep a backup of your entire website on a hard drive.

- **Your admin area should be secured –** The importance of your Admin area cannot be explained in words. It is THE most important part of your website because from here, you can access everything. Hackers often love to target WordPress sites. It is also true that several sites are up and running, and many of them haven't faced a threat in years. But in any case, a back up is essential to save you from any unforeseen circumstances. One of the first steps that you can take is setting up a firewall. Also, don't go for lame passwords. Use a combination of special characters, letters, and numbers, and make your password strong. You can also enable the two-step verification process to level up the security. So, even if someone does get your password, they will still require the authentication code to be able to log in to your account.

- **Keep an eye out for 404 errors** – These errors often lead to bad user experience and can really hamper your statistics. So, you need to make sure the proper functioning and loading of all pages and also eliminate any missing links that might be there. If your site is new, then the best way to ensure that there are no 404 errors is to manually browse it and see whether everything is normal and as expected. You can also set up email alerts for any such errors so that you can be notified at once and fix them as soon as possible.

- **There must be an email for your website** – One of the most common errors people face with their WordPress site is the inability to send or receive emails. Sometimes your email notifications might be working well and good and deliver properly, but sometimes they might not. This is mostly because of the incidences of email spoofing. When the email address of the sender is not matching with that of the originating server or domain, the mail servers consider it to be spoofing.

- **Check whether all the forms are functioning properly** – Once your email is set up, the next step is to check the forms on your website. Test all your subscription forms, contact forms, comment forms, or any other form that you have. Ensure that they are responding properly. You should also try and send some test emails to your mailing list to confirm that your emails are, in fact, being delivered properly. And if you are not building an email list, then you should start doing that right away. If your site is a multi-user one, then you should also keep a check on your Registration forms. The best way to do this is to log in to the account with different user roles.

- **For Ecommerce websites –** If you are running an eCommerce website, then user experience will form a very big part of it, and you also need to provide the best service at all times. Try browsing products by putting yourself in the shoes of the user. You can also make a test transaction by adding products to the cart and making a purchase. This will ensure that everything on your site is flawless, and your customers will not face any problems. In case you are selling digital goods, you need to check their prompt delivery. The process of completion of an entire order needs to be checked in case of physical goods.

- **All sliders, videos, and images need to be checked –** In order to make your website more interactive and eye-catching, the inclusion of videos, images, and sliders is necessary. But all of them should also be loading properly. Otherwise, there is no use of including them in the first place. In case you have implemented a Slider plugin, then you need to make sure that it is equally working on all browsers. The same goes for videos. You should try and play them on different devices and browsers to check how well they are functioning.

- **Social integrations need to be checked** – for a successful launch and performance of your website, social media integration forms a vital part. You should place buttons to connect to all platforms, including Twitter, Instagram, Facebook, YouTube, and so on. Also, all the social sharing plugins that you are using should be up and running.

- **Conduct performance tests** – You can use tools like Google Pagespeed to test the speed of loading of your website. Not only does a higher speed enhance the user experience, but it is also important for SEO.

- **Don't forget Google Analytics** – You need to know how your audience is interacting with your posts, and for that, you need Google Analytics. You need to install it before launching your website; otherwise, you will not be able to measure your performance and efforts. Also, you can keep a historical record of all your data so that after a couple of years, you can see how much your website has developed and grown.

Chapter 5: Working With a Default Theme

With every WordPress installation, you will get access to the Default theme too. This is nothing fancy but just a simple starter theme, and it is also enough to get your website up and running. The theme has a very clean and tidy appearance, and also, it has been designed in a way that most of the built-in display features of WordPress are utilized. All the features will be standard for your installation. With these features, you can even create your own header graphics, or you can even build your own Navigation menus by customizing the present one. This is done with the help of the Custom Menus feature.

The main advantage of working with the Default theme is that you will start getting a basic idea of how every feature functions in WordPress, and you will also get accustomed to them so that when you work with other themes, you are not going to face any problems. When you create your own theme, these same features will be present along with a lot of others as well. But when you use a Default theme first, you get the hang of things. All the information that you learn in this chapter has been carefully curated so that they apply universally to all themes. The Twenty-Thirteen default theme is usually advised for blogs or general websites because of its colorful approach and nicely laid out features.

The Layout and Structure

Millions of users on WordPress start with the Default theme, and it has a very simplified layout too. Also, you can customize pretty much everything on it. The layout might be simple, but it is also modern at the same time. The font that is selected is quite easy to read and sharp. The different features that are already built in the theme will help you make some elegant tweaks here and there and take your website to the next level. This also includes changing the background color of your website and also setting feature images of your choice.

The widget areas that come along with the Default themes allow you two layout choices which are mentioned below –

- **One-column layout** – This is the most popular layout for blogs and websites, and this is also the Default one that is selected with the Default theme. In this layout, there will be a Header area where your navigation menu and site title will be present. In the center of your website, there will be a content area. At the bottom of the website, there will be a Footer area, as well.

- **Two-column layout** – This layout is very commonly seen in websites and blogs, and you must have already seen it on the web. All the options that are already present in the one-column layout are present in this one as well. Additionally, you will get the option for a right sidebar where you can add all the required widgets.

In this Default theme, you will get two dedicated areas for your Widgets. One of them is the Main Area, and the other one is the Secondary Area. The footer region of your website is where all the Widgets of your

Main Area will appear. The right sidebar region of your website is the one dedicated to the Secondary Area Widgets. You will know all about Widgets later on in this book.

Customizing the Header Image

The image that appears on the top of your website is the Header Image, and most themes will have it. If you are using the Default theme, then everything is set for you, and all you have to do is to choose the image. Based on the built-in feature, you can either choose one of the three images provided, or you can also choose something of your choice by uploading it.

First, we will go through the steps you need to follow in case you want to select one of the header images that are already provided to you.

- **Step 1 –** Go to your Dashboard. From the Appearance tab, you need to select the Header option. On your browser window, you will find the Custom Header page opening. Among the header images that are already present, one of them will be selected as default, and you can see it in the Preview section.

- **Step 2 –** From there, you have to scroll to the portion which has the section of Default Images. Here you will find that usually, the first one is selected as Default. You can either change it to something else, or you can also set it to random so that every time someone visits your website, the image changes.

- **Step 3 –** Lastly, once you have made the changes you want, you need to click on the Save Changes button. This button is usually present at the bottom of the box. The page will then refresh itself, and your chosen option will be appearing in the Preview section.

So, whenever you want to make any changes to your Header image, you can simply revisit the Custom Header section and make the necessary changes.

Now that you know the basics, we will move on to the topic of how you can upload one of your own header images. This is important to know, especially if you want to make your site look unique and not something that everyone has. With these steps, you can upload any image that you have clicked yourself specifically for your website.

- **Step 1 –** Just like the previous procedure, go to your Dashboard. From there you have to go to the Header option which is present under Appearance. The browser will then load the Custom Header window.

- **Step 2 –** The next step is to scroll down to the section where you see the Select Image option.

- **Step 3 –** Once you reach that section, you will see a button named Browse, and you have to click on it. A dialog box will pop up in front of you, and it will give you the option to select a picture of your choice from your device.

- **Step 4 –** Now, you have to select the image of your choice from the folder in which it is present. Then you need to click on Open, followed by Upload and voila! Your image will be uploaded to the server. Then the Crop Header option will pop up in front of you.

- **Step 5 –** This step is optional, but for some, you will have to do it for aesthetics. 1600 x 230 pixels is the default size of the Header Image in the Default theme. If you ask my opinion, then it is always better for you to crop your image beforehand from some other image editing tool and then upload it. But in case you have uploaded the original image directly, then you can use the built-in tool for cropping that is present in WordPress. There will be eight small handles on your picture, and all you have to do is drag them to resize your picture. The picture will then be made of the required measurements, and you can safely upload it.

- **Step 6** – Then, once you have cropped your image to the required size, you have to click on the Crop button. Then click on the Publish option. The dashboard will reappear with the Custom Header box, and you can see your new Header image there.

- **Step 7** – Lastly, at the bottom, you will notice that there is a Save Changes option, and you have to click on it. The moment you do that, the image will be published.

Customizing the Navigation Menus

All the links displayed on your site are present in the Navigation menu, and as the name suggests, it helps the audience navigate through the website. With this menu, you can reach pages, posts, or categories that are published on the website. The built-in feature of WordPress makes customizing the Navigation menu quite an easier task.

To enhance the readability of your website, the presence of at least one Navigation menu is advisable. This way, your audience will know what your site includes and what it can offer.

So, if you want to create a Navigation menu in the Default theme, these are the steps that you need to follow –

- **Step 1** – As always, go to your Dashboard. From there, you will get the Menus option under the Appearance tab. Once you click on it, the page for Menus will open.

- **Step 2 –** Now, you will find a box called Menu Name. There you have to type the name of the Menu you want to create. Once you type the name, you have to click on the Create Menu button. After that, the page will refresh itself, and a message will be displayed on the screen saying that your New Menu has been created.

- **Step 3 –** Your next step is to add the links to your menu. Under the Pages tab, click on View All. When you do that, all the pages that are currently published on your website will be listed in front of you. Now, you have to decide which pages you want to include in that menu. If you want to include a certain page, all you have to do is check the box beside that option, and that page will be included. Then you have to select the Add to the Menu option. You can also add custom links. Firstly, in the URL box, you have to paste the URL of the website you want to include, and in the Label box, you have to include the name you want to be displayed. Then here too, you have to select the Add to the Menu option. Just like the pages, you can include Categories too by following the same procedure.

- **Step 4 –** Your next step is to review all the choices that you have made. The right-hand side portion of the box will have all the menus that you have created and also what you have included in it.
- **Step 5 –** You can also choose to edit the menu choices. This can be done if you click on the down arrow button that is present right beside the name of the menu.

- **Step 6 –** Once you have checked all the choices and you are satisfied with all of them, then you have to click on the option named Save Menu, and you will be done. When you have done that, a message will pop up on your screen, confirming that you have created a new menu.

Following the procedure that has been mentioned above, you can create any number of menus you want, and there is no limitation to it. Once you have saved your Navigation menu, you can also use several options to customize it the way you want and here are some of the things that you can do –

- **Rearrange the items in the menu –** You can rearrange the items displayed on the menu and arrange them in order of importance, alphabetical order or basically any order you want. And to do so, all you have to do is drag and drop the items on the Menu page. Drag the selected item to the desired position and then release your cursor to drop the item at the final position.

- **Creation of sub-pages –** If you are building a site that has lots of content in it, sub-pages can make it more orderly and easier for your audience to access the content that they want. To do this, you have to drag an item on the menu a little bit towards the right. But this item should be below the top-level item within which you are creating the sub-page. Another advantage of the sub-pages is that they prevent the Navigation bar from getting too cluttered. Once you have done the changes, simply click on Save Menu, and the changes will be saved.

With the default theme, all basic websites can be created. Moreover, in some manner, the default theme is also somewhat like a fallback theme in case your content and customized themes get deleted.

Chapter 6: How to Find And Install The Perfect WordPress Theme?

Selecting the perfect theme for your WordPress site can seem a bit difficult and overwhelming at first, but with this guide, it will all seem easier. You will get both paid and free options with WordPress, and all of them are wonderful. Every theme has its own uniqueness, but you have to go with something that suits you the best. So, this chapter is going to guide you along the path of choosing the perfect WordPress theme for your website. The Themes Directory page of WordPress is quite easy to navigate, and you can check out all the themes there. All the themes on the WordPress Directory page are safe and vetted for by the platform, which means they do not contain any malicious code and will not cause any spam either.

Things to Keep in Mind before Choosing a Theme

All types of websites can be made with WordPress, but the theme you choose should be able to convey the message for your website properly. There is a particular theme for every type of market and audience, and if you end up choosing the wrong one, you might not be attracting the right audience. In your quest to finding the perfect theme for your website, there are certain things that you should consider, and all of them are listed below –

- **Look out for simplicity** – You will find WordPress themes that are way too colorful with lots of animations and other features, which might sound cool, but in most cases, you don't really need all of them to make a website. So, what you need is a layout that will help you portray your website in the best possible light and also pave the stepping stones to your success. The simplicity, readability, and usability of your website should not be compromised at all costs while you are choosing a theme for your site. Also, you should bear in mind that the presentation style of your theme is very crucial and easy to understand. It should not be too complicated that people literally spend a long time what it is that you are trying to convey. The ultimate aim of any website design is to assist your audience in helping them find what they have been looking for and to provide them with the information they want in the easiest way possible. There might also be cases where the theme is really great, but it is not helping you in any way to grab a better quality audience or get more subscribers. In that case, the theme is not really working out for you. If your audience is not able to find their way around your content, then the theme is not good for you.

- **The theme should be responsive –** Do you know what it means to be responsive? Well, for starters, a responsive theme will always adjust itself on various screens or various devices. Thus, your content will appear as it is in both laptops and mobiles or even tablets. In today's world, a considerable amount of traffic comes from those who are browsing from their phone or any other type of handheld devices. Now the percentage of people browsing your website from a handheld device will also significantly vary with the kind of content you are producing and the audience you are targeting. You definitely wouldn't want these people to go back from your website just because it was not responsive, would you? Also, Google has a tendency to list mobile-friendly sites higher in search results. No matter what the demographics or statistics of your sites are, if your website is not mobile-ready or responsive, then you can forget about ranking higher on Google. Most themes that you get on WordPress are mobile-friendly, but there are also some in which the width cannot be properly adjusted. So, if you want to test whether your theme is responsive or not, here is a trick that you can follow. You can resize the screen of your browser, and if the theme adjusts itself, then it is mobile-friendly, and if it doesn't, then it is not.

- **Make sure it is browser compatible** – All users are not going to use Google. Everyone uses different browsers. Your theme might be looking just perfect on your screen because it is compatible with your browser. But for someone else, who is browsing on a different browser, the scenario may be completely different. So, you need to ensure that your theme is going to show the same performance on all browsers. Usually, sophisticated tools are used by WordPress developers to test the browser compatibility of the themes they launch. This is sometimes even mentioned. But just to be on the safer side, you can use basic tests of your own to check the browser compatibility. Simply launch the theme on different browsers apart from Google Chrome-like Safari, Firefox, and so on. Also, if you are testing these on your laptop, you also need to test the same on your mobile.

- **Check the plugins supported** – The WordPress plugins play a major role in the performance of your WordPress website. There are literally so many plugins to choose from, but there are some which are the basics, and you should definitely have them on your website. These are – Yoast SEO, Gravity Forms, W3 Total Cache, and so on. But in order to install them, you also need to make sure that the theme that you are choosing supports all of these plugins; otherwise, there is no use of that theme. If you are not really sure as to which plugins the theme supports, you can also raise a query with the developer.

- **Check for a theme that is translation ready** – Not all websites are translation friendly. But you will find so many websites on the internet that are in different languages other than English. And it is true that you can create such a website which is in some other language. If you are not creating anything like that now, you never know, you might want a multilingual site in the future. So, it is always better to choose a theme that allows you to translate and supports plugins of the multilingual category.
- **Pre-installed page builders** – These are a type of plugins in WordPress with the help of

which you can utilize a drag and drop mode to create the layout of your page. In the different premium themes of WordPress, these page builders come pre-installed, and this saves you from a lot of hassle as well. But in some cases, the page builders are not transferable as they are restricted to that developer only. In that case, if you ever decide to change your theme, you will have to go through a lot of hassle and clean up a lot of codes. So, choose your themes wisely, or you can get the page builders separately in order to use them with all themes.

- **Ensure that you get proper support –** It feels quite good to get a Free WordPress theme, but did you know that most of them do not have any Support option in case you are stuck in a problem? Yes, you heard it right. You will then have to figure out your own way, and that definitely is not something you want in the face of a severe problem. But with premium themes, you can get an excellent Support team backing you up in case of blockages. Sometimes not having a Support team means you might have to lose some cash to a developer to solve a problem, which was not even that difficult. So, whichever theme you choose on WordPress, it should come with ample support option for those days when everything seems to be going in the wrong direction. Sometimes, you can even get a year of email-based support in the premium themes, but you need to check this entire out before installing any of them.

- **Make sure the theme is SEO friendly –** The SEO friendliness of your website will be determined by a lot of factors, and your theme is a major one of them. A theme might be good looking from the outside, but in reality, it might be having a really poor HTML. So, you need to be aware of that, or your site's ranking and performance will be severely affected. If you are just a beginner in WordPress, then you might find it difficult to get the source code of your website all on your own. But with premium themes, you will find that in most cases, the developers mention it whether their themes are optimized for SEO or not.

- **Don't forget to check out the reviews** – The quality of any theme on WordPress can also be judged by the reviews and ratings. These are left by users, and so you can definitely put your trust in them. If a third-party marketplace has been used to sell the themes, then customer reviews will definitely be present there. In case the theme is free, then you will find an option for ratings right beneath the Download option. From there, you can see the number of users who have downloaded that theme and also the average number of stars left. If you click on the stars, suppose you click on five stars, then you will see the reviews of those users who had left five stars on that theme. You should also keep an eye out for bad reviews. If you find that the number of bad reviews on a particular is unusually more than the usual amount, then you should better steer clear of that theme.

Steps to Install a Theme on WordPress

Now that you know all about the things to consider before choosing a theme, it is time that you learn how to install a theme. The process is quite simple.

Step 1 – You can either search for a particular theme, or you can browse through the list, and when you reach the one you want, you need to download the Zip folder of that theme on your device.

Step 2 – Then go to your Admin area. From there, you need to go to the Themes page from the Appearances tab.

Step 3 – On the top region of the Themes page, you will find an option called Add New. You have to click on it, and you will be automatically directed to a page where you can add new themes. At the top of this page, you will find the Upload theme button, and you need to click on it.

Step 4 – The theme upload box will appear on the screen in front of you. There will be a Choose File button on which you have to click. Then you have to browse the zip file that you had initially downloaded on your device. Select that Zip file and then choose the Install Now option. The theme will then be uploaded from your computer to WordPress.

Step 5 – Once the installation is done, a success message will pop up on the screen in front of you. And there, you can find two options – activate the theme and preview the theme. If you are planning to activate it right then, you can preview it first and check whether everything is the way you wanted. If everything is fine, then you can activate it, and it will start functioning on your website.

In case you are using Free themes, you can install them very simply and without any hassle. These themes are absolutely free, and there is no two way to this. But they sometimes lack certain things which are essential to expanding your website and so you need to be careful about that. The Premium themes will cost you some money, and you can download them only after you have paid the amount. They can be as low as $10 or as high as $500. It all depends on how much you want to invest.

Chapter 7: All about Widgets

If you have completed the book up to this point, then you already know the basics, and now it is time for you to know more about widgets. They will make your site more attractive and also enhance readability. These are small blocks that perform different functionalities, and they can be added to the sidebars of your website. The sidebar region of your website is also known as the widget-ready portion.

Originally, these widgets were launched with the aim of creating a design that will be easy to use and also has a simple structure. This gives the user better control over their own website. Operating the widgets is quite easy too. You can simply drag and drop them in the area where you want, and you are good to go. If you want to know what all widgets are present in WordPress, you can simply click on Appearance on your Dashboard and then go to Widgets.

In the digitized area, you can add several features and specialized content of your choice. The area dedicated to widgets in your theme may not be the same as the person next to you. The sidebar is one of the most common regions, but it doesn't mean that it is the only region. For your theme, it can also be the header, footer, or basically any other region of your website. The widget available to you will also not be constant and vary from one theme to the other.

Mostly, themes have more than one widget area, and they are all widget ready. But there is no hard and fast rule about having widgets, and so your theme is not required to have a widget in order to run. Thus, you might not always find a widget with your theme. In case you do not see any widget area, then you have to understand that your theme doesn't have one.

Widgets can be of different types. The default WordPress comes with widgets like a tag cloud, categories, search, calendar, Navigation menu, recent posts, and so on. Suppose you want to install the categories widget in your widget area, then all you have to do is drag and drop it in the area you want, and it will start showing the calendar on your website.

Adding Widgets?

There is more than one way to add your widgets to the sidebar of your website. As already mentioned above, the drag and drop process is the easiest. You simply have to drag the desirable widget onto the sidebar. But there is another way in which you can do it. For that, you have to go to the list of available widgets, and from there, you have to click on the title of the desired widget. When you do that, WordPress will automatically start showing you the sidebars where you can place that widget. Then, you just have to select the one where you want to place the widget, and then you will find an Add Widget button. You have to click on it, and your task will be done.

But in case you find it challenging to use the drag and drop interface, then there is another way of adding widgets, and that is by using the Accessibility mode. Here are the steps for adding widgets through this mode.

Step 1 – Start off from the Admin area, and there you have to go to Appearance and from there to Widgets.

Step 2 – Once the Widgets box opens, you will find a Screen Options tab on the top of the screen. You can either click on the tab, or you can press L on your keyboard. If you press L once, you will be directed to the Help tab above the Screen Options tab. If you press L twice, you will be taken to the Screen Options tab, and then you have to hit Enter.

Step 3 – The Screen Options tab will then show its options, and there is only one it, and that is the Enable Accessibility mode. The moment you click on it or press Enter, the mode will be activated. The Widgets will be reloaded on your screen but in a new interface.

Step 4 – In this new interface, you will see the Widgets with a special Add option just beside their title. When you click on this option, a single page containing your widget will open where you can configure the rest of the settings.

Step 5 – Here, you can choose which widget area you want for your widget, whether it is the sidebar or something else. There is also a Position menu that you will find, and this menu helps you select the position within a particular widget area.

Step 6 – Once you are done with adjusting all the Settings, there is a Save Widget button on which you have to click, and you will be automatically taken back to the previous screen. When you are in the accessibility mode, the existing widgets will start showing a separate Edit button beside their title. If you click on that Edit button, the screen for edit widget settings will open, which is the same as the previous one you visited.

So, that's all, and in this way, you can add any widget you want to your website.

Removing Widgets

Now that you know how to add widgets, you should also know about the process of removing widgets.

Step 1 – For this too, you will have to start from your admin area. From there, you have to go to the Widget option, which is present in the Appearances tab.

Step 2 – Your next step is to look for the widget you want to delete. Once you find the desired widget, click on its title, and it will expand.

Step 3 – At the bottom of the settings, there is an option to Delete the widget. But you have to remember that if you click on this option, the widget will be completely removed from the area along with all its settings.

Step 4 – If the widget is a complex one, then it will have a lot of settings, and losing them would mean that you will have to do it all over again in case you feel like adding that widget later in the future. On the other hand, there are widgets that are way too simple and do not have any such settings. If your idea is to remove a widget without deleting any of its settings simply, then you can drag the widget in question and drop it in the section of Inactive widgets. When you do this, the widget will still remain in your available widgets section, and so, you can add it whenever you feel like it in the future.

List of Some Useful Widgets on WordPress

If you are just a beginner and not aware of some of the most useful widgets on WordPress, don't worry because I have prepared a list for you.

- **WP Call Button –** The traffic generated from mobile users is growing with each passing day, and this has made it even more important to place a WP Call button because most people today want to get more information about your business through a call. This widget will allow you to add a special button to your website – Click to Call Now. And the best thing about this is that you do not need a developer or any coding skills to it. You will also get endless options for customizing this button based on your business requirements. Also, this widget is totally responsive, and so it will look equally great on all devices. With any business, it is of utmost importance that you create as many leads as possible, and that is why this widget allows you a special option too. You can add a smart floating call button to your website. This means that the button will scroll as the user scrolls your page. There are four layouts of sticky buttons that you can choose from. They also provide you with a built-in tracking system, so if you use the widget along with Google Analytics, you will be able to track the source, which is generating maximum phone calls.

- **WPForms –** If there is a perfect contact form widget for WordPress, then it is WPForms. With this widget, you can create a contact form, and you can place it at any place you wish on your site. If you are going to write a code for an online form, it is going to be really hard, but with this widget, you do not require any codes. Your form will be created in a few minutes. Whether it is an online survey, donation form, or any other type of form, you need not worry at all. Also, to ensure a user-friendly process, the widget comes with pre-installed form templates. So, if you are short on time, you don't necessarily have to start from scratch. From multi-page forms to file uploads and even radio buttons, everything is accessible through this widget. So, if you want to integrate these forms with some email marketing service, you can easily do so. You can even choose to collect payment for orders and bookings. The widget also has been programmed to prevent any spam form submissions. With these forms, you can view all your leads under one roof.

- **RafflePress** – If you are planning to conduct a giveaway and make it viral, then RafflePress is the widget you need. With this, you can attract a lot of traffic at once. The giveaway builder has a drag and drop interface, and so you won't be facing any problems while building your attractive giveaways. All you need is just a few minutes, and you do not need to hire a separate developer for this. There are several in-built templates that you can use to speed up the process as well. This will help you grow your traffic and also enhance your engagement levels. This widget is 100% responsive and thus will work the same way in all other devices as well. One of the biggest problems faced during giveaways is tackling fraud entries, but with this widget, you can handle that too. The one-click entry feature of the widget keeps your contest fair. You need to supercharge your growth if you want to attract a larger audience, and this widget will automate the entire process of word of mouth marketing. The amazing social media integrations of this widget will help you in sharing your giveaway on all social media channels, as well. The widget will also give you a seamless email marketing integration so that you can grow your mailing list. The tracking feature of the widget, along with its retargeting tools, can definitely place a great impact on your conversion statistics. The giveaway landing page creation is quite easy, and you can create a distraction-free page for your viewers that will result in the best outcome.

- **Recent Posts** – The Recent Posts widget is already present in WordPress, and you should definitely add it. But if you want a better-looking widget, then you should consider adding the Recent Posts widget with thumbnails. This will not only give you a list of your most recent posts, but they will also display thumbnails, post titles, excerpts, and so on. For the thumbnail, it is usually the first image of the post or the featured image that is used. From the widget settings, you can customize the widget by adjusting its height and width according to your requirements.

- **Astra Widgets** – This is basically a widget pack, and you will also find a theme in WordPress that goes by the same name because it is created by the same developers. But you should know that this widget will work perfectly with any theme of your choice. The most wanted information for any kind of website is those of your list icons, social media profiles, and also your business address. With this widget pack, you can create widgets for all of this information on any place on your website. Having the best coding standards, this widget pack can really provide a faster performance to you. Also, you can do a lot of customization that, too, in a few clicks. You can use this widget with any of the major page builders, and it will work seamlessly without any glitch at all. If you want to minimize your overall design time, don't worry because there are so many ready-to-use website demos with these widgets that you can simply install.

- **Social Media Icons** – Social media is so important in today's world, and if your posts cannot be shared on social media, they will not receive the exposure that you were hoping for. And adding social media icons to your website is quite easy if you have the right widgets for it. All you need to do is install the Simple Social Icons plugin and then follow the steps mentioned here. After installing the plugin, you have to go to the Widgets window from the Appearances tab in your admin area. From here, you can drag and drop the Widget in your desired location, preferably your sidebar. Then, you can also customize several things like you can configure the colors, size, and alignment of these social icons. To make the icons work, all you need to do is add the link to your social media profiles. All the popular social media platforms are supported by this widget, and some of them include Google+, Twitter, Facebook, LinkedIn, Instagram, Pinterest, and so on. After you have entered all the desired URLs, you simply have to click on the Save Changes button and Preview it to see how it looks on your website. If they do not look good, you can try them out with different background colors of your choice.

- **Google Maps –** This widget is also one of the most important ones to add to your website. For this too, you will have to install the Google Maps Widget plugin first. Then you have to go to the Widgets window from the Appearances tab in your admin area. Then just like with other widgets, you have to drag and drop the widget in the area you want to place it in. Now you have to enter the address. This is the address that you want to show on the map and so make sure you enter the correct one. Here, you can also choose other factors like the zoom level, pin color, and the map size. Then you have to click on the tab marked lightbox and configure the respective settings there. Once you are done, you can click on the Save button, and your Google Maps widget will be ready to use. Using this really helps the audience because they do not have to search you on the map manually. All they have to do is click on the map from your website and then track their way down.

- **Social Count Plus** – If you have already established a considerable amount of followers on social media, then it is advisable that you display them on your website as well because it will fetch credibility in the minds of your audience. This is direct social proof. With the help of the Social Count Plus widget, you can show the number of followers or subscribers you have on the respective social media channels. Once you install the plugin, you have to go to the Settings and then to Social Count Plus.

There you will see boxes for each social media channel, and you will have to paste the link to your profile in each of these boxes. The widget has different types of button designs that you can choose from. If you are not satisfied with the color of the text of your follower count, you can change it too. All of this can be done from the Design tab of the widget. But remember, this widget is only meant for the purpose of showing your follower counts and not the share counts of your post. There is a different widget for the number of times your posts have been shared.

- **Compact Archives –** WordPress already comes with an Archives widget, but this does not have too many options. With this, you can only display your monthly archives in the form of post links. But just imagine when, after a few years, you have so many months of content, and your archive will simply become too long to navigate. Yes, there is, of course, an option for a drop-down menu, but there is a disadvantage to it. Your Archives will become reduced and thus not grab much attention from the audience. The Compact Archives widget can be quite helpful in this scenario. This widget has the ability to group your archives in different years and thus show you a tidier and more compact version. You can add it to your site's About page, to your sidebar, or even create a completely separate section for Archives only.

- **Testimonials Rotator –** Having social proof is of utmost importance to create an impression among your first-time audience. This widget is specially meant to add customer testimonials to your website in a well-laid out manner. The best thing about this widget is that they can create rotating testimonials for you. Also, you can choose how it rotates, the animation, and even the duration that you want to give to each testimonial. There will be two default themes included within the plugin, but if you want more, you can purchase them separately.

So, now that you know about all the important widgets for your site, you can include the ones you need, and your audience will experience better navigation across your website. Keep experimenting with different widgets because there is no end to them and see what works best for you. Also, you need to have some content for some widgets to work, for example, the Recent Posts widget. If you don't have posts yet, this widget will not display itself.

Chapter 8: How to Use The Different Plugins?

If you want to enhance the visual appeal of your WordPress website, plugins will be your best friend. They offer solutions based on very specific issues, for example, social networking, web forms, or even email marketing. Plugins are not something necessary, but using them will definitely benefit you a lot. In the Plugin Directory page of WordPress, you will find that there are many plugins that are completely free while there are the Premium ones that are paid. The paid ones definitely come at a nominal cost, but they also perform complex functions. Here, in this chapter, you will learn about both free and paid plugins of WordPress.

Steps to Install the WordPress Plugins

In this section, you will learn all about finding the plugins, downloading them, and also how to install and activate them.

How to find free plugins?

In this first section, we will learn about how you can find the best yet free plugins. You can find them from your Dashboard itself, and the process is very easy. You have to select the Plugins option, and from there, you will find another option called Add New. Click on this option. There you will find a dedicated search box where you have to type the term and then select the Search Plugins option. This will list those plugins which match your term exactly.

There are different tabs present on the top of the Install Plugins page, and these are as follows –

- **Search** – This is the default view, and in this tab, you can search for the plugins by using various terms of your choice.

- **Search Results** – This tab is not present at first but appears once you have conducted a search. This is the tab where you will get all the results for your search using any particular keyword.

- **Upload** – In this tab, you will get the necessary options to upload a plugin on WordPress directly.

- **Featured** – As the term indicated, here you will find the Featured plugins or the ones which WordPress thinks are perfect for your use. In short, these are the major plugins that every admin should check out.

- **Popular** – This is basically a list of those plugins which are currently more popular according to the WordPress criteria.

- **Newest** – As you may have already guessed, this tab will show you a list of all those plugins which have been recently added to the pool.

- **Favorites** – You have the option to mark plugins as your favorite in the directory. So, this tab basically shows you the list of those plugins which you had marked favorite.

But one thing that is common with all of these tabs is that with them, you will be introduced to so many different plugins that you can try out without actually searching for them. So, you must always explore all these tabs because you never know what you may find. Sometimes, you might end up stumbling upon some plugin that you didn't know about but is useful to you.

At the bottom of this page, you will see a different section. This section will have a selection of keywords in it. So, when you select one of these keywords, all the plugins that are listed under this keyword will be shown to you. For example, if there is a keyword called gallery and you click on it, then every plugin that is related to the gallery in some way or the other will be listed in front of you. In short, if you want to search for popular plugins, then you can use keywords of your choice as well.

How to install and activate a chosen plugin?

If you have already found the desired plugin, then the next step is to install it.

Step 1 – There will be a Details tab beneath every plugin. So, when you have set up your mind regarding a plugin, and you want to install it, click on this Details tab that you will see on the Install plugin page. It is usually present beneath the title of the plugin. Then you will see that the more information dialog box opens in front of you. Here, you will find all the details about the plugin. But sometimes you might also get a message which would tell you that the plugin has not yet been tested with the WordPress version that you currently have. This happens because the plugin's author might not have updated it to run on the latest version of WordPress. So, the options open in front of you are – you can either install it and see if it works, or you can contact the author and ask them to update it.

Step 2 – Once all of this is sorted, you will notice that at the top region of the dialog box, there is an

Installation tab. You can have to click on it, and all the details regarding the installation will be shown to you. You should always go through all the instructions before proceeding with anything. The activation and installation process of every plugin differs from the other in some way or the other.

Step 3 – Then you need to go to the Description tab, and from there, you will get the Install Now option. You have to click on it to install the plugin. The page of the Install plugin opens after the previous dialog box closes. Then a message will be shown to you regarding the success of the installation.

Step 4 – Then you will see that a link with the text – Activate Plugin – appears on your screen. If instead of this, anything else appears, or some mishap occurs during the installation of the plugin, you have to click on the Help button and then proceed with the steps mentioned there. You should keep a note of any error message that pops up on your screen.

Step 5 – In order to ensure that the Plugin was, in fact, installed correctly, you should click on the

Plugins option from the Dashboard. The plugins page will open, and if your plugin was installed correctly, you would see it on that page.

How to manually install a plugin?

The previous method that was mentioned was easy, but the manual installation of plugins is not a cakewalk. But the previous method will work only in the case of Free plugins from the directory. If you wish to install any commercial plugins, which you will have to do at some point in time, you will have to know about the manual installation method. This requires you to do it via File Transfer Protocol or FTP. The steps for manual installation of a plugin are as follows –

Step 1 – The first step is to download the plugin on your device from the source, obviously. You will get download links from the commercial developers, which will directly download the plugin when you click on those links. But the files of the plugin are usually downloaded in a Zip format.

Step 2 – So, the downloaded files will be in a compressed folder. You have to extract the files.

Step 3 – Use your preferred FTP application to connect to your server.

Step 4 – The next step is to find the folder of the wp-content.

Step 5 – Now, you have to search for the plugins directory in the wp-content directory. It is here that you have to upload your desired plugin, and you have to do it with the FTP application. Once that is done, your plugin will be successfully installed. And now, all you need to do is to activate it.

Step 6 – Go to your Dashboard and then select Plugins from the Plugins option. The page of Install Plugins will open.

Step 7 – You will find the activation link below the name of your desired plugin. You have to click on this link.

Using E-Commerce Plugins

In today's world, everyone starting from individuals to businesses, is turning to the world of the internet to expand their business and reach greater goals. This will also increase your profit margins by bringing in an extra chunk of money. And so, WordPress has several E-commerce solutions for those who are looking forward to expanding their business outlook. With WordPress, creating content and publishing it happens in the blink of an eye. And along with that, you can also use some create plugins that will boost up your product sales. But first, you need to understand how E-commerce plugins can help you out.

Here are some things that an e-commerce plugin will help you with –

- Create your own store of products where you can list everything
- Display products with alluring and attractive images
- State the price of each product along with its name
- Configure shipping rates and sales tax

- Get inventory tracking features
- Make space for payment gateways like Google Checkout or Paypal so that your audience gets the chance to purchase something directly from your website
- And so on.

Some of the common products that you will find people selling on WordPress sites are as follows –

- **Downloadable digital products** – software or ebooks
- **Physical products** – clothing, jewelry, handmade home décor items, digital equipment
- **Memberships** – member-only websites, societies, clubs.

Creation of Portfolios or Photo Galleries

You must have seen those amazing sites which have impactful photo galleries. So, do you want one for yourself? This is quite important, especially if your work involves you displaying some of it to your audience or creating a visual impact. This is most commonly used by logo designers, web designers, photographers, and so on. You might also find bakeries having a photo gallery because how else will the customers know how good and unique their products are. Well, there is no end to the number of people who might require a portfolio. There are several plugins that you can use to build your portfolio or photo galleries.

Creation of Web Forms

In most cases, you have to create a way for your visitors to contact you. But you cannot post your email id directly on your website because this will increase the chances of spams and bots attacking you with useless emails. So, it is not advisable for you to post your email address publicly. Instead, what you can do is create a form for your visitors, which they can fill and email you. These are called contact forms. When visitors come to your site, and they have any questions, they can simply fill out these forms and get the answer from you. Here, the visitor will be including their email address, name, reason or concern, and a detailed message. In this way, you can respond to them directly, and at the same time, you are not revealing any email addresses directly on the web. This will keep your mail safe and away from the reach of bots and spams.

So, now you will learn about the common type of forms that you can include in your website with the help of plugins –

- **Order Forms –** In this form, you can collect all the information you need from your customers. You can include all the necessary fields of information that you need, and your visitor will be filling them up in order to contact you. This is very commonly used in companies who want to know certain things from a client before they place an order. So, when a client is seeking a quote for a project, they will have to fill-up the form and thus give you some information about them. This will help you understand what the client actually needs.
- **Surveys –** This is another very common type of form that you will see on the web, and with this, you can collect reviews about certain services or

products. With these forms, you can also collect certain testimonials for your business.

- **Lead-Generation Forms** – These forms can help you gather valuable information about your customer base and readership. These forms are not considered to be spam because people fill them out willingly and only if they want to. This will also assist you in making a list of potential contacts to which you can send newsletters and updates.

Chapter 9: Top 10 Important Plugins For WordPress

In the previous chapter, you have learned all about adding and installing plugins, and now, here, you will learn about the most important plugins that you should definitely install.

Yoast SEO

This is probably the most popular plugin in WordPress and for a good reason. With the help of this plugin, you can bring in more audience to your website from all other search engines. It is true that the setup of WordPress is extremely SEO friendly, but to make it work, you also need to take some steps on your own to boost the SEO. And so, Yoast SEO is here with a comprehensive solution to all your problems. It is quite easy to use too. You have to enter those keywords for which you want your site to rank on the search engines. Then the plugin will run a search for you. They will tell you whether you are using the over popular keywords and whether you are using the keywords in the right position.

Also, Yoast SEO will not only check the word that you have entered but every variation of that word or phrase as well. Suppose your keyword is 'best hotels in Miami,' then the synonymous term for this phrase is 'top Miami hotels.' Apart from the synonymous variation, Yoast will also take into consideration the separate words of the phrase. In this way, you are indulging in some core SEO optimization. They also have an amazing Redirect feature, and it is quite helpful too because, with it, you can create as much as 301 redirects.

MonsterInsights

This is one of the best Google Analytics plugins you will get in the market. All you need is to go through a few steps, and your universal tracking across all platforms will be up and running. Also, your website analytics report will always be right in front of you on your Dashboard. You can also get access to real-time stats and thus see who is online at that moment. You will also be able to see what that visitor is doing. You will get a very detailed report of your stats, and this can be generated for each post and page as well and not only for your website as a whole.

There is a special Affiliate link tracking feature with this as well. So, you can keep track of your banner ads, affiliate links, or any such thing. In the audience report of the plugin, you will be able to see a lot of things, including the device that your audience is browsing from, the country where they are in, and also their gender, age, and much more. All of these insights will definitely be useful in terms of improving your web strategy.

Sucuri

Having proper security should always be your top priority because you definitely wouldn't want all the hard work that you have put in your site to vanish just because of some hacker. This plugin will provide you with a web application firewall. It also considered being one of the top security plugins you can get for your website. They have the ability to remove any type of malware from your site safely. If there is any malicious code in your database, Sucuri will detect it and remove it at once. They even perform removal of blacklist status on your behalf. In case your site gets blacklisted for some reason, 95% of its traffic will be lost, but don't worry as Sucuri will take care of it.

Link injections and spam keywords can cause harm to your site's performance. But Sucuri can fix it for you. Hackers keep trying every day to find out some vulnerability of your site. But this plugin is experienced in removing threats on a daily basis. DDoS or Distributed Denial of Service often leads to downtimes. But Sucuri has the ability to block layers 7, 4, and 3 of any such DDoS attacks.

Akismet Anti-Spam

If you want to keep all the spammers at bay, then Akismet Anti-Spam plugin is the one you need. They have a global database of spam, and all your contact form submissions and comments will be checked against that database by this plugin. This will eliminate any chances of you publishing any malicious content by mistake. And it does all of this automatically so that you do not have to face any hassle at all. They also provide a status history for everything so that you know which comments were found to be spammy. The best thing is that it is free to download for personal sites, and even if you are getting the premium version, it is quite affordable.

WooCommerce

Offering you a plethora of features, WooCommerce has become immensely popular among all e-commerce websites. It is completely customizable and thus trusted by everyone all over the world. If you are someone who wants to venture into the unconventional world of eCommerce solutions, then WooCommerce is exactly what you need. This one plugin has been found to be powering over 34% of the sites on the web. Also, you can stay assured about security as the plugin is audited by Sucuri from time to time. From digital downloads to physical products, you can sell basically anything and everything you want.

Being open-source, you get endless options for customization with the WooCommerce plugin. You can take unlimited orders and list unlimited products because everything is in your own hands. You can pick from countless themes, all of which are cool and colorful. You can also get the option to display the customer reviews directly on the product page. You can also offer your customers with one-click refunds, and all of this can be directly managed from the dashboard of WooCommerce. In case there is a critical stage in order, you can send personalized notes to your customers too.

LiveChat

If you have an e-commerce or business website, then you should definitely get LiveChat as it is one of the top live chat support plugins you will get. Also, it can provide you with an endless number of customization options, and on top of that, you will also be getting a mobile app. This will help you stay connected while you are outside or traveling. The plugin will automatically detect some of the actions that your audience is taking on your website and customize some invitations based on that action. You can also create a custom eye-catcher, which will ensure that your visitors can always notice the chat window on your website. There are certain ready-made eye-catchers that you can use, or you can also make your own one and upload it.

You can also create a canned response so that you do not have to enter the same answer multiple times. So, all you need is a few keystrokes, and your answer will be ready. This can save a lot of your time. Apart from this, with the LiveChat plugin, you will get access to the necessary visitor information that you can use to close sales or even resolve a support case. You can also send more intuitive, appealing, and customized answers to the questions your visitors ask. You can also exchange files with your audience with the LiveChat feature because it will provide you with a simple drag and drop window. You can access all these chats later on, too, because they will be stored in the archive.

Nextiva

With this plugin, you will get a separate business phone number for your website. This number will come with unlimited domestic calling, call routing, voicemail to text or email, and even online faxing. If you do not want to be disturbed at odd hours, then you can set up your own business hours with this plugin as well. They also have other communication features, like online surveys and CRM. No matter through which channel you are communicating, you can keep track of all your conversations through this one plugin.

When you jump around to a number of tools, it will only take up a lot of your time, but with Nextiva, you are getting everything under a single roof. You can track and measure everything, and so with the help of Nextiva's analysis, and you will know how your customer is feeling about your services. With the historical insight that Nextiva gathers, you can cater to the individual needs of every customer in real-time.

Jetpack

This plugin basically performs a variety of functions and not just a single task. It will provide you with a variety of site management tools to enhance your site's performance. There will be no storage limits, so you need not worry at all. This multi-featured plugin is trusted by businesses and personal blogs alike. Also, this is one of the most well-maintained plugins you will get for WordPress. Some of the common things that you will be able to perform are monitoring downtime so that you get instant notifications when your site is down, adding contact forms, and also including social sharing buttons on your site so that your viewers can share your content.

The addition of this plugin will also protect you from hackers so that they cannot force themselves on your login page. It will also reduce your bounce rate and work on increasing your engagement by showing posts that are related. It will also take the daily back-up of your blogs. Auto-publicizing your blog posts is also possible with Jetpack. If you use Jetpack, you can actually reduce the number of plugins in use because Jetpack has a comprehensive list of functionalities.

Contact Form 7

When it comes to contact plugins, you literally have thousands of options, but Contact Form 7 is one which is widely trusted by others. It is also very simple to configure. Simple markup is all you need to customize the forms according to what you want, and you can also handle multiple forms in a single place with this plugin. Another important feature is that it supports Ajax-powered submitting. With this form, your users will also be asked to fill in their referral source, and so you will have the information as to how your audience is learning about you or how they are navigating to your website.

With this plugin, you can skip all the extra coding required to set up a contact form and quickly come up with beautiful and unique contact forms for your audience. There are over 1100 5 star reviews for this plugin and over 5 million active users. You can also steer clear of any spammy submission because the plugin is filtered by Akismet.

WordFence Security

If you want to protect your site against vulnerabilities, then getting WordFence Security is a must. Cyber-attacks are proliferating at a very high rate, and so you need to take measures accordingly. An endpoint malware scanner and firewall are present in this plugin, and the plugin is always programmed with the newest firewall rules and malicious IP addresses. There is a bad history associated with cloud firewalls, and they can be very easily bypassed. But with this plugin, there is no need to break end-to-end encryption. The scanner identifies and blocks all those requests which contact the malicious codes.

It also has options like limited login attempts and thus prevents all brute force attacks. It also works with the user to enforce stronger passwords. The scanner does a thorough check, including code injections, bad URLs, malicious redirects, and SEO spam. All the known vulnerabilities are also checked, including the closed and abandoned plugins. The analytics will also show you real-time hack attempts, including their IP addresses. They also have a leaked password protection feature, which prevents admins logins that are happening with compromised passwords. They also have a country blocking feature with the help of which countries are effectively blocked when they are reported to have engaged in malicious activities. The plugin uses the source code verification to assist you in after hack recovery. It will also give you notifications regarding what all has changed in your plugins, core files, and themes.

Chapter 10: A Complete Guide to User Roles In WordPress

WordPress user roles are something you probably never thought of if it was only you who was responsible for running the website, but when you are doing it with others, you definitely have to think about what task you are delegating to whom. And that is where the purpose of roles comes in. When you set these roles, you can control what access you are giving to whom, and then that person cannot do anything else apart from the access given to him/her. The assigning of user roles in WordPress not only helps in streamlining your workflow but also ensures that your site is safe and secure.

There are several sites that have multiple users, and all of them have their individual accounts. This can get really complex, and you definitely do not want to end up giving access to something to someone who shouldn't be accessing those in the first place. Suppose you are building a website, and there are separate users who are working on each part of the content, then it is definitely a good idea to restrict some of the admin as well as editing capabilities. But how is that possible? It is possible with the feature of user roles in WordPress. If you want to collaborate with your team members in a better way without actually imposing any risk to your site whatsoever, then setting user roles should be your first priority.

In this chapter, we are going to learn all about the user roles, how are they set, and how you can adjust the different permissions as well.

An Introduction to the Concept of User Roles

Well, to explain it in the simplest way possible, anyone who has a WordPress account would be called a user. This means users can be anyone from team members to employees, as well. For example, if you are creating the new content for your blog and you have several editors and writers working for you, then it is highly likely that all these people will have their own account.

Also, members of your community can be users too. If you have an e-commerce website, then you might be allowing your customers to create their own accounts so that they can do certain important things like track their orders. On the other hand, when it comes to forums, if people want to post messages, they usually have to sign up.

So, it doesn't matter who the user on your site is but every user has his/her own role to play. So, if you assign them these roles, they cannot go beyond the boundaries and handle something they aren't supposed to. Some of the usual tasks included in the different roles include –

- Mentioning the sections of your site that these users can gain access to in the back end
- Access to the changes that they can make like altering settings or changing plugins
- Restriction on the content type they can create, delete or edit

But the most important and common role is that of the administrator. The person who possesses the role of an admin is the one who can do anything and everything with the site literally. All the other roles, except for that of the Administrator, are restricted to some extent.

Importance of Roles in WordPress

Now that you have a basic idea about the roles, you might be wondering why do these exist in the first place. Couldn't everyone be accessing anything and everything they want? The simple answer to your question is no, and if you read on, you will understand why. There are a number of vital reasons for which the set of roles is important.

Some of the primary reasons for this the user roles are crucial are as follows –

- Security risks are reduced to a significant extent, especially when your account is being handled by multiple people. This is because you can straightaway deny access to certain important things in your account and keep those actions limited to yourself. Or, you can allow those settings only to the most trusted users.

- Sometimes, even well-meaning users might end up making some mistakes. But with the role setting features, these mistakes can be avoided. One of your writers might be accidentally deleting a post, which was crucial to your site. Or, someone might uninstall an important plugin by mistake. But you can prevent all of this by restricting their access to these parts.

- With role setting, you can come up with a prominent and clear hierarchy for your website. This is highly crucial for when multiple users are working with your account.

- This also acts as a good work strategy. When users are performing well or have proved themselves to be trustworthy, then you can promote them to roles that allow them more access or give better privileges. This, in turn, will keep them motivated, increasing the overall productivity of your website.

- You can use the feature of assigning roles with other features like plugins. There are different types of plugin that can create a method for you, which will allow you to add restricted members-only content on your website. And then, you can use the role setting feature to decide who will constitute the restricted members club.

So, do you understand now why setting roles is important? If you do, then it is time for you to understand a few basic things related to this concept.

Default Roles in WordPress

There are six default user roles in WordPress. You need to know about what these roles are before you get into any more details.

Super Admin

So, the first and most important role that we are going to speak about is that of the Super Admin. But this is a bit different from the other. Do you know why? It is because it only applies to the setups of WordPress Multisite. This is a special feature with which you get the liberty to handle several websites from one single account. Thus, you can connect all of these sites together, which makes them more manageable but at the same time, give each of them the autonomy they deserve.

But, remember that if you are only running a standard website on WordPress, the Super Admin does not apply to you. This role becomes crucial when we are speaking about a Multisite setup. In short, the person who has this role will get full access to all the sites present in the network.

Some of the functions that Super Admin can do are as follows –

- Delete and also create websites
- Manage plugins or add or remove plugins in the network
- Handle every aspect of the themes
- Manage the overall working of the sites and also assign different user roles

Now, you definitely understand by all this how important and powerful the Super Admin is. But you also need to keep in mind that with this immense responsibility, it is always better to have only one person, that is the owner of these sites, at this role.

This is because the person who is holding the rank of Super Admin is the one who will be handling everything happening in the network, and as far as individual website management is concerned, all of that can be left to the Administrators.

Administrator

If you are running a standard website, that is, a non-multisite feature, then an Administrator will always be at the top of the hierarchy. All authoring privileges, along with everything that goes on in the back end, is in the control of the Administrator.

Some of the functions that the Administrator can do are mentioned below –

- Modify or create or delete content from the site
- Manage the settings
- Handle the user accounts
- Update the themes, core files, and plugins from time to time
- Edit all files
- Export as well as import content
- Remove and install themes and plugins

Here too, it is important that you keep only on Administrator for your website. This is mainly advised with the aim of eliminating the risk of security breaches. Also, you can reduce the rates of contradictory and unintended changes. But in case you simply have to set more than one Administrators for your site, then make sure that you keep the number to a minimum and also ensure that the people to whom you are granting this power are fully trustable.

Editor

Just like the editors in a physical company, the Editor of a WordPress website is responsible for overseeing the content part. Some of their functions include –

- Edit or even create posts and pages too along with other types of content
- Publish, edit or delete content that has been made by other users of the website
- Manage links, categories, and comments

All the administrative aspects of the site are not given to an editor. They will not be allowed to install themes or plugins or process any updates. They will also be restricted from the Settings section so that they cannot make any changes to them. You should try and keep your pool of editors limited, too, but in any case, there are very minute risks with the role of an editor.

Author

As you can understand from the term itself, an author is a person who gets the right to create content and also to publish it. Some of the important functions include –

- Edit, create, publish, or delete your own posts. But they cannot do anything to the pages
- Responsible for the uploading of media like videos or photos and also access the Media Library

But one thing that you should get clear is that no author can make any changes to the pages. If you are working with a huge team of content creators, then having a team of authors will be of great help. And when it comes to an author's own work, they do not need any approval to publish it. So, learning about the next few roles is very important.

Contributor

This is nothing but a scaled-down form of the role of the author. Some of the tasks a contributor does are explained below –

- Edit and create posts of their own but not publish them. They can send the posts for review
- View each and every post on the website including those that have been created by others
- Delete the posts that have been created by them

One thing that you need to get clear is that no contributor is able to publish any type of content. Someone like the editor or anyone higher than the contributor has to first go through the content and then decide whether to publish them or not. Also, no content can be uploaded by the Contributors to the Media Library.

So, this is what makes the contributors a very important role, especially a one-time role. Or, you can also make a writer a contributor in the beginning in case they are not yet trustworthy for all sets of permissions. Also, if you have hired any new writers, then you should consider assigning them to a contributor position first and then promote them to become an author because, in this way, you can create a work-based motivation in them.

Subscriber

Last but not least comes the subscriber. This is the most restricted role out of all the other roles. The only thing that a subscriber on your site can do is read content and nothing else. Thus, all your pages, posts, and everything else can be viewed by them. And, they can handle their own user profiles, but apart from all of this, nothing is given access to them.

You might now be thinking about what the point of this role is if they cannot really do anything. But this role has a use too. If your site has a membership factor, then you will have to create subscribers, too, and this is exactly where this user role will come of use. You can either restrict some of your content to a subscriber, or you can restrict all of it. It is completely your option. But even if you are not creating any membership component, then this particular option can help the visitors manage their own profiles. In short, you never know when it might come handy.

How to Manage User Roles?

Now, it is time for you to know how you can manage different user roles. The first step is to know how and where you will find them on your WordPress site. Well, but you also need to understand that it is only the Super Admins and the Administrators who can access this section. So, first, make sure you have one of these roles. If you do, they follow the steps mentioned here.

Step 1 – From your admin panel, go to the option Users and from there go to All Users.

Step 2 – Now, you will be able to see on your screen, a list of all the users on your site. Each of the users will also have some kind of role attached to their name. If you want to edit any of those roles, then you will find that besides their username, there is an option called Edit. You have to click on it.

Step 3 – The moment you click on Edit, a box appears, and from there, you have to scroll down to the role option you want to set. Select the option.

Step 4 – Save the changes.

So, once you have ensured that all the roles have been assigned properly, your next step is to set the default role. Go to Settings. From there, go to the General Settings. There you will find an option New User Default Role. Usually, it is advised that you don't select anything higher than a Contributor.

How to Create Custom User Roles?

By default, WordPress has set the capabilities of each. But not only can you edit the capabilities of a current user role, but you can also create your own user role as well. But for that, you need to get the Capability Manager Enhanced plugin.

Once the plugin is installed, go to Capabilities from Users option. Then, you simply have to select the user role that you plan to edit. Then after selecting the user role, you have to select the load button. The capabilities will be listed in front of you. So, if you want to remove any of the capabilities, you simply have to uncheck them from the box. Then click on the Save Changes button.

But you can also create your own role. In the Capabilities dialog box, you will see a box named Create New Role. In there, you have to enter the name of the role you want — for example, support staff. Then you can assign the capabilities you want that role to contain. Once you have created the role and assigned the capabilities, you simply have to save the changes and you are done.

Chapter 11 – How To Create Your First Post On WordPress?

So, if you have read all the chapters till now, then you are quite ready to launch your first chapter on WordPress. In order to make sure that you do not find it overwhelming, we have literally covered every aspect of all the previous chapters. In this chapter, we have made a comprehensive guide on how you can utilize all the features on the new post screen and publish your first post.

Add the Title to Your Post and Content Blocks

The block editor of WordPress has a very clear interface, and it is quite easy to use as well. Right at the top, you will find the space where you have to enter the title of your post.

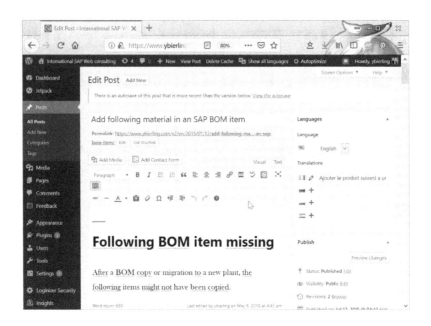

Then, in order to add more content to your post, you will first have to insert a block. You will find Add Block buttons on the editor screen itself, and they are in the form of plus signs. All you have to do is click on them. Every content element that can be added in WordPress is present in the block. For example, columns, paragraphs, galleries, images, shortcodes, embeds, widgets, and so on. Also, if you are using the WordPress plugins, then some of them may add some extra blocks to the editor like SEO, contact forms, and so on.

Add Media

Your next step is to add some media and spice up your content to make it attractive. For example, if you want to add some image, then you have first to select the image block, and then the upload image dialog box opens. From there, you either have to select one of the images already uploaded or upload a new one.

In case you want to take it a bit more further, then you can add both text and image aligned side by side. For this, you have to select a different block – the Media & Text block. With the help of this block, WordPress will assist you in wrapping the image around your text.

But you will find another block in WordPress that can come of help to you. And that is the Gallery block. In case you want to create a full display of all the images, for example, if you are creating a display of your work, then this block is what you need. You can arrange your pictures in columns and rows in the layout of a grid. And all you have to do is add the Gallery block, and then, as usual, the Upload image box will open from where you either have to select the images you want or upload new ones.

The Gallery block is definitely a powerful option, but for more specifications, you should get the WordPress gallery plugins with the help of which you can get image sorting features.

The editor also provides embed blocks for all the latest and common providers. For example, if you want to include your YouTube video, all you have to is copy and paste your URL in that box. But you can also use the video block in case you want to upload videos to your site directly.

Add Tags and Categories

You can sort your posts with the help of tags and categories. They are like taxonomy, and with them, you can organize your website into various topics and sections. This also boosts your overall SEO performance. Your audience stays pleased as well because they do not have to waste time in finding the content they were looking for. On the right-hand side of your window, you will find both the categories and tags options, and they are present under Document Settings.

Add a Featured Image

A featured image can also be called the post thumbnail, and it is important to have one. This image should be selected carefully as it is the one that will represent your entire content in that particular blog post. For all single posts and archive pages, this is the image that will be listed along with the title of your post, so the image should be able to create an impression on the mind of the audience. The featured image functionality is supported by almost every WordPress theme. On the right-hand side of your screen, you will notice Document Settings, and under it is the option of Featured Image.

If you click on the button 'Set Featured Image,' a window will open, and you can select a picture of your choice or even upload a new one. But you should not be confusing yourself between cover images and featured images as both of them are different concepts.

Add an Excerpt

An excerpt is like a summary of the article or the blog post but in a short format. Usually, the WordPress themes will generate the excerpt for you by combining the first few lines of your posts. But the excerpt that is created automatically is not always so meaningful and is not able to catch the audience's attention. So, it is advised that you create your excerpt manually. Under the Document Settings, you will find a separate box named Excerpt. You have to type it down there.

Change the Permalink

Even if you do not create your Permalinks manually, WordPress will create a URL automatically for you that is SEO-friendly. The post's title is the default permalink. But in case you want to make the permalink more SEO optimized, then you can do so by changing it. You can do so in two ways.

If you click on the title of your post, there will be an option to change the permalink. But you will also find that the Document Settings has a separate Permalink tab, and if you click on it, you can change the Permalink from there as well.

Change the Author

If your WordPress site has multiple authors, then it is useful to know how you can change the author's names of posts. In the Document Settings option, you will find an option called Status and Visibility. You have to click on it. Under this heading, there will be an Author option. There you will get a drop-down menu from which you have to select the desired name as your author name for that post. Then you have to click on the Update button to make the changes.

Turn Comments Off or On

There is a built-in commenting system in WordPress. With the help of this system, your audience is free to leave their comments on your post. But in case you do not want the commenting on a particular post, you can turn it off. Under the Document tab, there is an option called Discussion. If you click on it, there are two options. In case you do not want comments, you can uncheck the box of Allow Comments.

Learn About the Publishing Options

Now, we have covered all the basics for your WordPress post. Moving on to the publishing options, you will see that the edit screen of WordPress has two columns. You write your content on the left-hand side column. And on the right-hand side column are all the Settings options. There you will also find the Publishing Options. Here is what you will find there –

- Suppose you are composing a WordPress post, but you do not want to complete it in one go. That is when you will need the Save Draft option. All the changes that you make are also saved automatically by the editor.

- There is also a preview button with the help of which you can see how your post will appear once you have published it. This will take you to a new browser tab.
- If you have completed all the edits to your post, then it is time for you to click on the Publish button, which will make your post public.
- You also get multiple visibility options for your post on WordPress. The public is the default option selected, but you can change it to password-protected or private as well.
- You can also decide when you want to publish the post. Publish Immediately is the default option selected, but you can also schedule the publishing. You can select not only a future date but also a past one.
- There is another option called Stick to FrontPage. It basically does what it says. If you check this box, then your post will become a Featured one, and it will be displayed on the Home page. Also, it will appear on the top.
- If you have a multi-author blog, then you can make use of the Pending Review option. The

person will be able to save the post until an editor edits it.

- In case you want to delete a particular post, there is a Move to Trash button on which you can click. But remember, that even if it is done accidentally, all the deleted posts stay in the trash folder for a period of 30 days so that you can retrieve it later if you want. But after that period of time, it will be permanently deleted.

Conclusion

Thank you for making it through to the end of *WordPress For Beginners: A Visual Step-By-Step Guide to Mastering WordPress*, let's hope it was informative and able to provide you with all of the tools you need to achieve your goals whatever they may be.

I hope now you can implement everything that you have learned and finally make your first blog post. This book has been compiled in a way that can be useful to everyone, including those who are building e-commerce sites to those who have a personal blog.

Do you know why WordPress is so popular among everyone? Well, the first and foremost reason is that it has an amazing set of tools for users. These tools can help you with every task at hand. But make sure you maintain consistency. If you are not consistent with your blogs, they will not be performing well.

Also, make complete use of the plugins to ensure that your posts are SEO optimized and also include social sharing buttons to expand your reach and popularity. This is no rocket science, so if you keep learning something new each day, and you will be mastering WordPress by the end of the month. With WordPress, you can build a community and share your story. Familiarize yourself with the platform, and don't be afraid to explore the options; otherwise, you will never know about the several features that WordPress has to offer.

Finally, if you found this book useful in any way, a review on Amazon is always appreciated!